Flower Garden

Mosaic **Blanket**

Crochet a Garden for Your Home!

A crochet pattern by Erin Toews

Juniper & Oakes

This book is dedicated to:

My Mother

for teaching me to crochet.

Table of Contents

Hi! I'm Erin.

I learned to crochet when I was just a little girl. I remember sitting beside my mother watching her crochet me a rainbow scarf in treble crochet and wanting to give it a try! She taught me & I forgot. And she taught me again & I forgot, again. Finally in high school I picked up my hook and never put it down! Crocheting has gotten me through many tough times, and I am happy to bring crochet patterns into the world that help others get through their hard times as well.

This Mosaic Flower Garden Blanket crochet pattern is made using the overlay mosaic crochet technique. And if you've never tried this style of crochet, you are in for a real treat!

This pattern was born out of a desire to use the mosaic charts I created for my Monthly Mosaic Mystery CAL (a free crochetalong I ran in 2022 on my blog) and create a different blanket with a cohesive theme. The Flowers and the Lattice patterns were in the MMMCAL, and the two butterfly patterns were designed specifically for this blanket. The blanket was released as a premium crochetalong in the Spring of 2024, and then it had a second run in Spring of 2025.

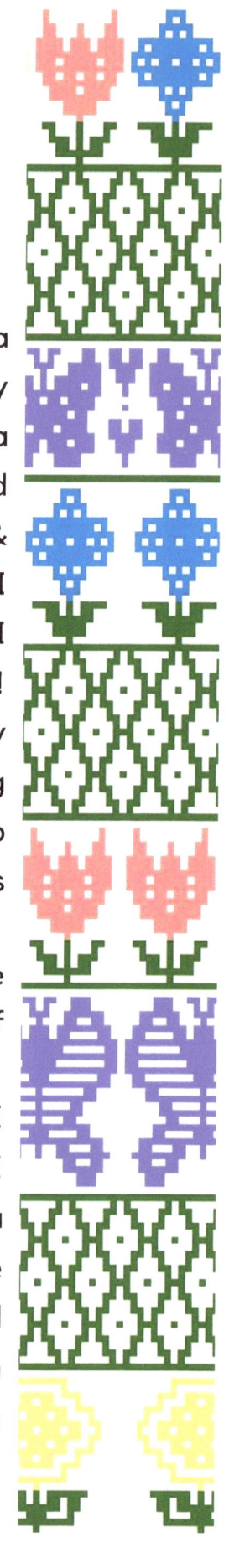

This pattern definitely looks more intimidating that it actually is. All it basically consists of is two basic stitches, single crochet and double crochet. You work one in the back loop of the stitch and the other in the front loop left behind two rows down. That might not make much sense reading it in this introduction, but I have pictures and video links to help walk you though it. There is even a "cheat sheet" in the back of the book that you can cut out and set it beside you wil you crochet, so you don't miss a thing! I always say that the hardest part about mosaic crochet is telling yourself that you should just give it a try. Once you pick up your yarn and make a small swatch, you'll be hooked in no time!

If you happen to get stuck somewhere along the way, take a picture of your project and post it with your question in the Juniper & Oakes Crochet Community Facebook Group. The crocheters in that community are so helpful and knowledgable; we'll sort you out in no time.

You are always welcome to email me personally My email address is erin@juniperandoakes.com. Please just remember that I am a "hot mess mama" and it might take a few days for me to respond.

Scan the QR code to join the FB group!

Scan me

Happy Crocheting!

Details

Skill Level: Adventurous Beginner/Intermediate

Materials

- **Yarn:** Mary Maxim Maximum Value, medium #4 yarn
  (100% Acrylic; 474 y/445 m per 8 oz/227 g skein)
  - Cottonwood (Color A) - 2515 yards/6 skeins
  - Medium Green (Color B) - 860 yards/2 skeins
  - Yellow (Color C) - 300 yards/1 skein
  - Medium Violet (Color D) - 555 yards/2 skeins
  - Medium Rose (Color E) - 300 yards/1 skein
  - Medium Denim (Color F) - 300 yards/1 skein

  or any #4/Medium Weight Yarn in 6 colors

- **Hook:** H / 5mm
  G+/4.5mm for the border
- Scissors
- Yarn needle

Gauge:

15 stitches x 18 rows = 4" x 4" in square
A swatch of the pattern

Finished Size:

Approximately 58" x 66"

Purchase the Yarn Bundle

Scan me

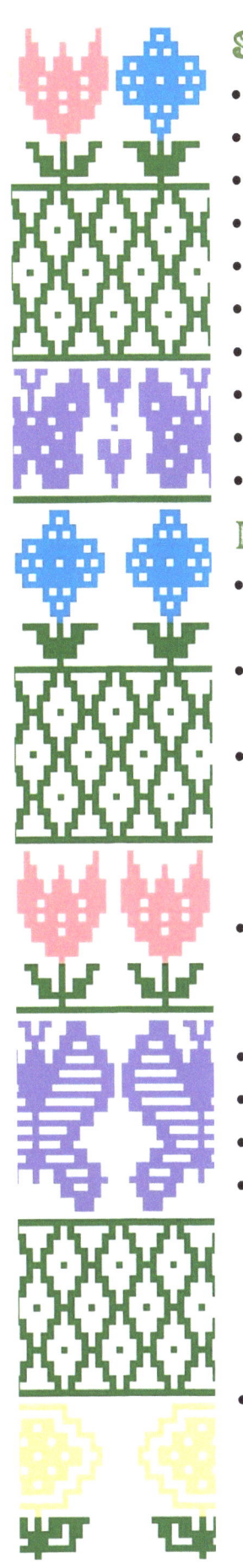

Stitch Abbreviations (US Terminology)

- ANC-FLOdc - Anchored FLO Double Crochet
- BBS - Beginning Border Stitch
- BLOsc - Back Loop Only Single Crochet
- ch - Chain
- EBS - Ending Border Stitch
- FLOdc - Front Loop Only Double Crochet
- Fsc - Foundation single crochet
- lp - Loop
- RS - Right Side
- sc - Single Crochet

Chart

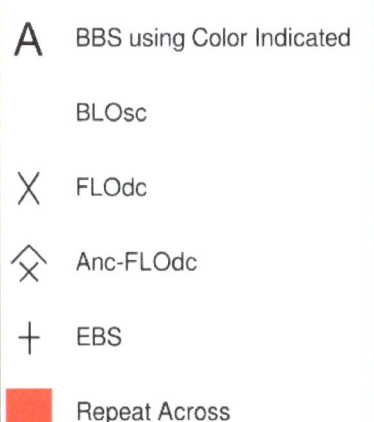

A	BBS using Color Indicated
	BLOsc
X	FLOdc
◇	Anc-FLOdc
+	EBS
🟧	Repeat Across

Pattern Notes

- Pattern is worked from right to left on RS only. (If you are left handed, feel free to work from left to right).
- Every row is worked in a different color. The WS will look like stripes.
- Fasten off at the end of each row. Do not turn your work. Begin next row where the previous row began. This creates a million little ends - *do not weave them in*. We will create an envelope border at the end of the project to hid those ends.
- Repeat the pattern as many times as you wish. The Foundation Row is made up of any multiple of 48 plus 3 extra stitches. I used 4 repeats, so mine is (4x48) + 3 = 195 stitches).
- The patterns include a chart and written instructions.
- The colors on the chart indicate how the finished project will look.
- Color B is used first so the background color is Color A throughout.
- Section 9 is worked using multiple colors on the contrast color rows. Carry all 3 color strands along with each stitch. Note how the FLOdc stitches in this section are Anc-FLOdc to ensure the unworked strands are secured along the rows. Change back to Color E before each repeat.
- The pattern can be worked up in two colors. Simply ignore any other color changes and alternate your Color A & B throughout.

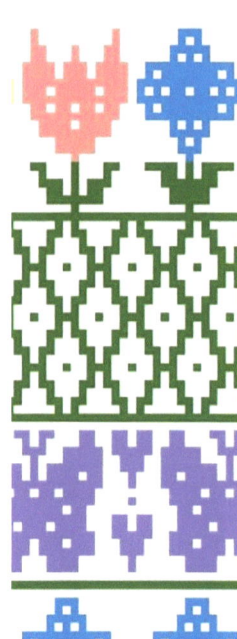

Special Stitches

Overlay Mosaic Technique

If unfamiliar with the technique, you should practice with a small swatch first so that you get comfortable with the different stitches before diving headfirst into a large blanket project. A swatch pattern and video tutorial can be found after the description of the special stitches. If you need more resources, take a look at the mosaic crochet section of the Juniper & Oakes website, and watch the video playlist for this blanket.

More Resources for Mosaic Crochet

Scan me

Video Playlist for this Blanket

Scan me

Beginning Border Stitch (BBS)

A standing sc through the post (or the 'v') of the stitch below, ensuring that both legs of the stitch on the WS are to the outside of the blanket. *(For right-handed crocheters the legs would be secured to the right of the stitch and vice versa for left-handed crocheters.)*

Back Loop Only Single Crochet (BLOsc)

Insert hook in back loop of indicated st, yo and pull up a lp, yo and draw through both lps on hook.

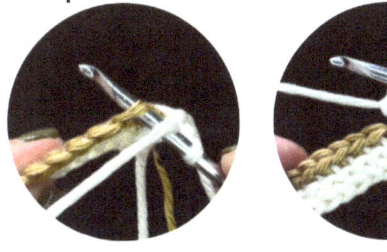

Front Loop Only Double Crochet (FLOdc)

Yo, insert hook in front loop of st below the indicated st, yo and pull up a lp, yo and draw through two lps on hook, yo and draw through remaining two lps on hook.

Ending Border Stitch (EBS)

A sc through the post (or the 'v') of the stitch below, ensuring that both legs of the stitch on the WS are to the outside of the blanket. (Similar to BBS, but the back legs of the stitch are secured to the opposite side.)

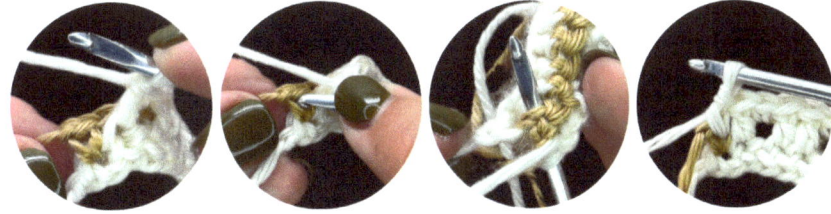

Anchored FLO Double Crochet (Anc-FLOdc)

With unworked yarn carried across the stitches, insert hook in BLO of indicated stitch and draw up a loop, YO, insert hook in FLO of stitch one row below SAME stitch and draw up a loop, YO and draw through 3 loops on hook, YO and draw through remaining 2 loops on hook.

Swatch Practice

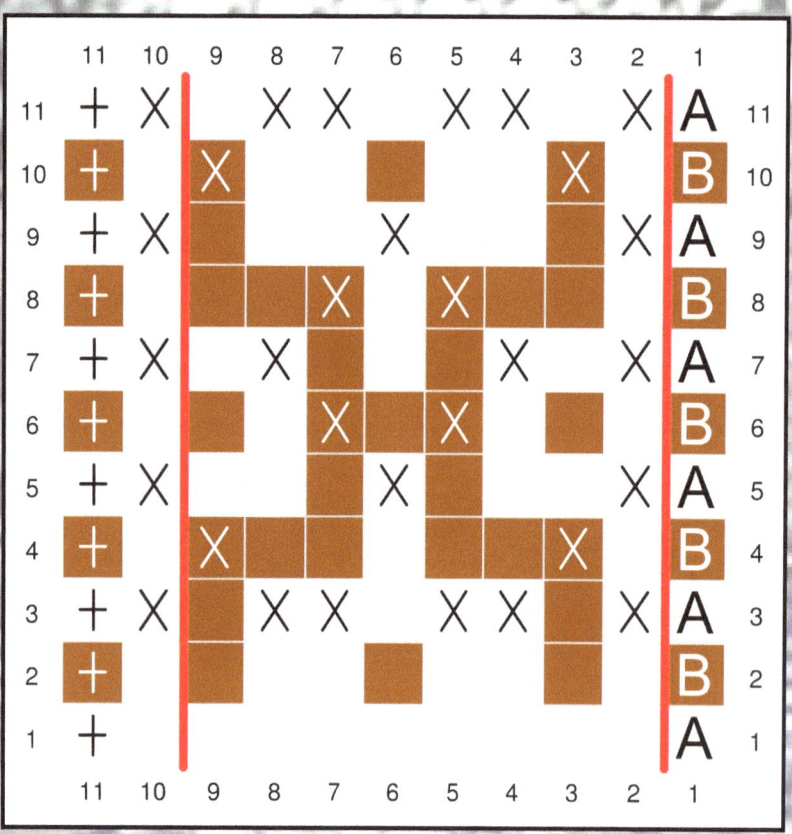

	11	10	9	8	7	6	5	4	3	2	1	
11	+	X		X	X		X	X		X	A	11
10	+		X			▪			X		B	10
9	+	X	▪			X				X	A	9
8	+		▪	▪	X		X	▪	▪		B	8
7	+	X			▪		▪		X	X	A	7
6	+		▪		X		X				B	6
5	+	X				▪	▪		X		A	5
4	+		X	▪	▪				X		B	4
3	+	X		X	X		X	X		X	A	3
2	+		▪			▪			▪		B	2
1	+										A	1
	11	10	9	8	7	6	5	4	3	2	1	

Legend:

A	BBS using Color Indicated
	BLOsc
X	FLOdc
+	EBS
▪	Repeat Across

Video Tutorial

Scan me

Swatch Instructions

Row 1: With Color A, Fsc 11 (or any multiple of 8 +3).

(Alternatively: Ch 12, sc in 2nd ch from hook and in each ch across.)

Row 2: With Color B, BBS in 1st, BLOsc across, EBS in last.

Row 3: With Color A, BBS in 1st, *FLOdc x1, BLOsc x1, FLOdc x2, BLOsc x1, FLOdc x2, BLOsc x1*, repeat across, FLOdc x1, EBS in last.

Row 4: With Color B, BBS in 1st, *BLOsc x1, FLOdc x1, BLOsc x5, FLOdc x1*, repeat across, BLOsc x1, EBS in last.

Row 5: With Color A, BBS in 1st, *FLOdc x1, BLOsc x3*, repeat across, FLOdc x1, EBS in last.

Row 6: With Color B, BBS in 1st, *BLOsc x3, FLOdc x1, BLOsc x1, FLOdc x1, BLOsc x2*, repeat across, BLOsc x1, EBS in last.

Row 7: With Color A, BBS in 1st, *FLOdc x1, BLOsc x1, FLOdc x1, BLOsc x3, FLOdc x1, BLOsc x1*, repeat across, FLOdc x1, EBS in last.

Row 8: With Color B, BBS in 1st, *BLOsc x3, FLOdc x1, BLOsc x1, FLOdc x1, BLOsc x2*, repeat across, BLOsc x1, EBS in last.

Row 9: With Color A, BBS in 1st, *FLOdc x1, BLOsc x3*, repeat across, FLOdc x1, EBS in last.

Row 10: With Color B, BBS in 1st, *BLOsc x1, FLOdc x1, BLOsc x5, FLOdc x1*, repeat across, BLOsc x1, EBS in last.

Row 11: With Color A, BBS in 1st, *FLOdc x1, BLOsc x1, FLOdc x2, BLOsc x1, FLOdc x2, BLOsc x1*, repeat across, FLOdc x1, EBS in last.

Simple Chart of Complete Blanket

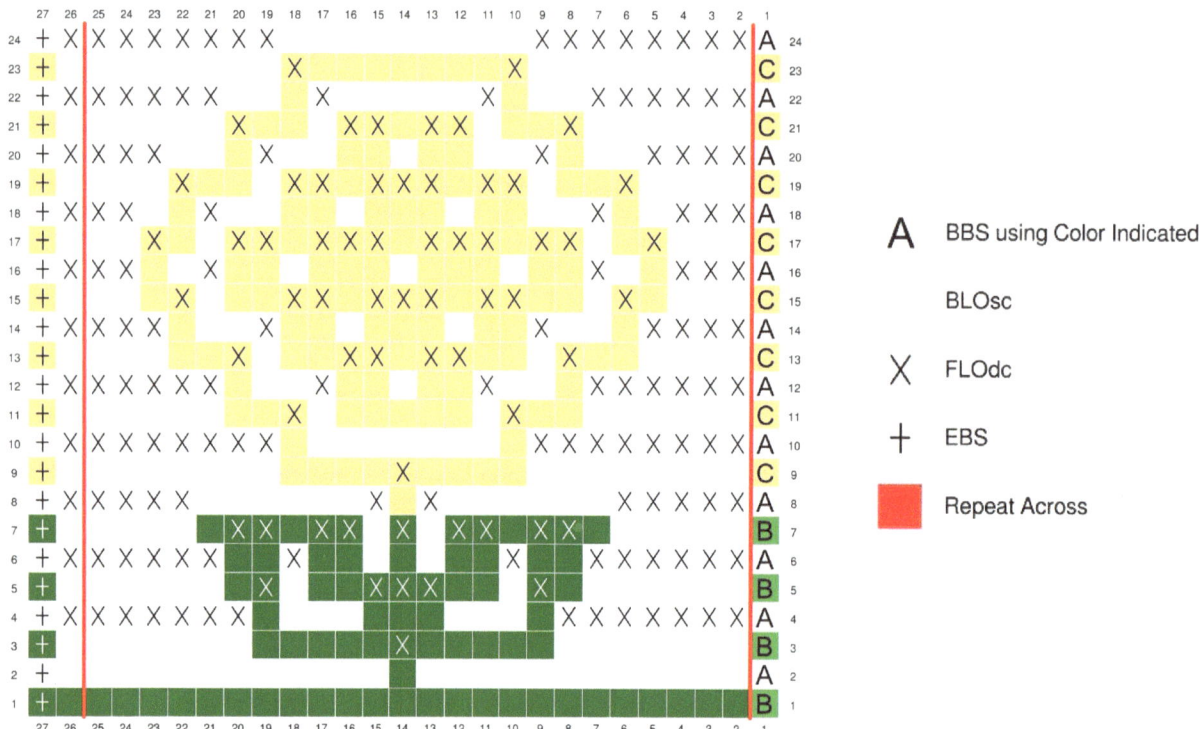

	Symbol	Meaning
	A	BBS using Color Indicated
		BLOsc
	X	FLOdc
	+	EBS
	🟥	Repeat Across

Foundation Row: With Color B, Fsc 195 (or any multiple of 48 +3).

(Alternatively: Ch 196, sc in 2nd ch from hook and in each ch across.)

Row 2: With Color A, BBS in 1st, BLOsc across, EBS in last.

Row 3: With Color B, BBS in 1st, *BLOsc x12, FLOdc x1, BLOsc x11*, repeat across, BLOsc x1, EBS in last.

Row 4: With Color A, BBS in 1st, *FLOdc x7, BLOsc x11, FLOdc x6*, repeat across, FLOdc x1, EBS in last.

Row 5: With Color B, BBS in 1st, *BLOsc x7, FLOdc x1, BLOsc x3, FLOdc x3, BLOsc x3, FLOdc x1, BLOsc x6*, repeat across, BLOsc x1, EBS in last.

Row 6: With Color A, BBS in 1st, *FLOdc x6, BLOsc x2, FLOdc x1, BLOsc x7, FLOdc x1, BLOsc x2, FLOdc x5*, repeat across, FLOdc x1, EBS in last.

Row 7: With Color B, BBS in 1st, *BLOsc x6, FLOdc x2, BLOsc x1, FLOdc x2, BLOsc x1, FLOdc x1, BLOsc x1, FLOdc x2, BLOsc x1, FLOdc x2, BLOsc x5*, repeat across, BLOsc x1, EBS in last.

Row 8: With Color A, BBS in 1st, *FLOdc x5, BLOsc x6, FLOdc x1, BLOsc x1, FLOdc x1, BLOsc x6, FLOdc x4*, repeat across, FLOdc x1, EBS in last.

Row 9: With Color C, BBS in 1st, *BLOsc x12, FLOdc x1, BLOsc x11*, repeat across, BLOsc x1, EBS in last.

Row 10: With Color A, BBS in 1st, *FLOdc x8, BLOsc x9, FLOdc x7*, repeat across, FLOdc x1, EBS in last.

Row 11: With Color C, BBS in 1st, *BLOsc x8, FLOdc x1, BLOsc x7, FLOdc x1, BLOsc x7*, repeat across, BLOsc x1, EBS in last.

Row 12: With Color A, BBS in 1st, *FLOdc x6, BLOsc x3, FLOdc x1, BLOsc x5, FLOdc x1, BLOsc x3, FLOdc x5*, repeat across, FLOdc x1, EBS in last.

Row 13: With Color C, BBS in 1st, *BLOsc x6, FLOdc x1, BLOsc x3, FLOdc x2, BLOsc x1, FLOdc x2, BLOsc x3, FLOdc x1, BLOsc x5*, repeat across, BLOsc x1, EBS in last.

Row 14: With Color A, BBS in 1st, *FLOdc x4, BLOsc x3, FLOdc x1, BLOsc x9, FLOdc x1, BLOsc x3, FLOdc x3*, repeat across, FLOdc x1, EBS in last.

Row 15: With Color C, BBS in 1st, *BLOsc x4, FLOdc x1, BLOsc x3, FLOdc x2, BLOsc x1, FLOdc x3, BLOsc x1, FLOdc x2, BLOsc x3, FLOdc x1, BLOsc x3*, repeat across, BLOsc x1, EBS in last.

Row 16: With Color A, BBS in 1st, *FLOdc x3, BLOsc x2, FLOdc x1, BLOsc x13, FLOdc x1, BLOsc x2, FLOdc x2*, repeat across, FLOdc x1, EBS in last.

Row 17: With Color C, BBS in 1st, *BLOsc x3, FLOdc x1, BLOsc x2, FLOdc x2, BLOsc x1, FLOdc x3, BLOsc x1, FLOdc x3, BLOsc x1, FLOdc x2, BLOsc x2, FLOdc x1, BLOsc x2*, repeat across, BLOsc x1, EBS in last.

Row 18: With Color A, BBS in 1st, *FLOdc x3, BLOsc x2, FLOdc x1, BLOsc x13, FLOdc x1, BLOsc x2, FLOdc x2*, repeat across, FLOdc x1, EBS in last.

Row 19: With Color C, BBS in 1st, *BLOsc x4, FLOdc x1, BLOsc x3, FLOdc x2, BLOsc x1, FLOdc x3, BLOsc x1, FLOdc x2, BLOsc x3, FLOdc x1, BLOsc x3*, repeat across, BLOsc x1, EBS in last.

Row 20: With Color A, BBS in 1st, *FLOdc x4, BLOsc x3, FLOdc x1, BLOsc x9, FLOdc x1, BLOsc x3, FLOdc x3*, repeat across, FLOdc x1, EBS in last.

Row 21: With Color C, BBS in 1st, *BLOsc x6, FLOdc x1, BLOsc x3, FLOdc x2, BLOsc x1, FLOdc x2, BLOsc x3, FLOdc x1, BLOsc x5*, repeat across, BLOsc x1, EBS in last.

Row 22: With Color A, BBS in 1st, *FLOdc x6, BLOsc x3, FLOdc x1, BLOsc x5, FLOdc x1, BLOsc x3, FLOdc x5*, repeat across, FLOdc x1, EBS in last.

Row 23: With Color C, BBS in 1st, *BLOsc x8, FLOdc x1, BLOsc x7, FLOdc x1, BLOsc x7*, repeat across, BLOsc x1, EBS in last.

Row 24: With Color A, BBS in 1st, *FLOdc x8, BLOsc x9, FLOdc x7*, repeat across, FLOdc x1, EBS in last.

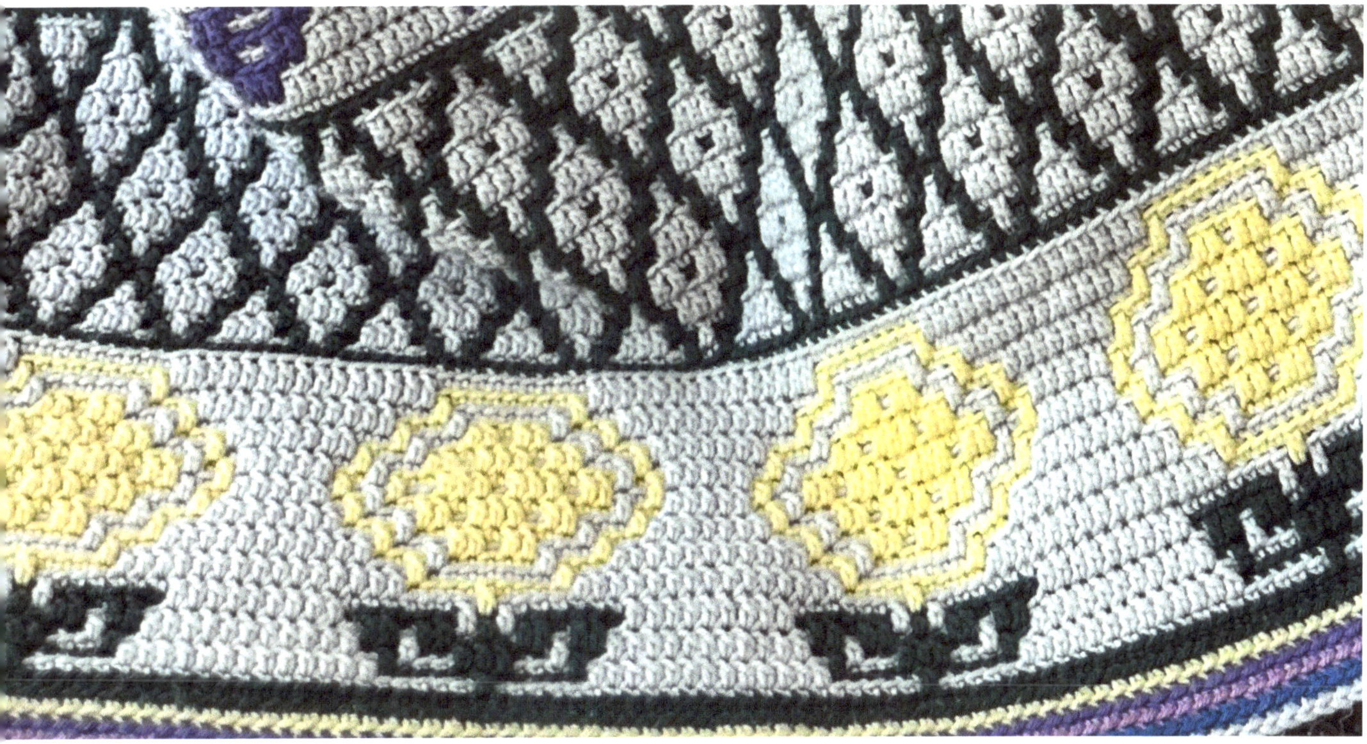

Section 2-Lovely Lattice

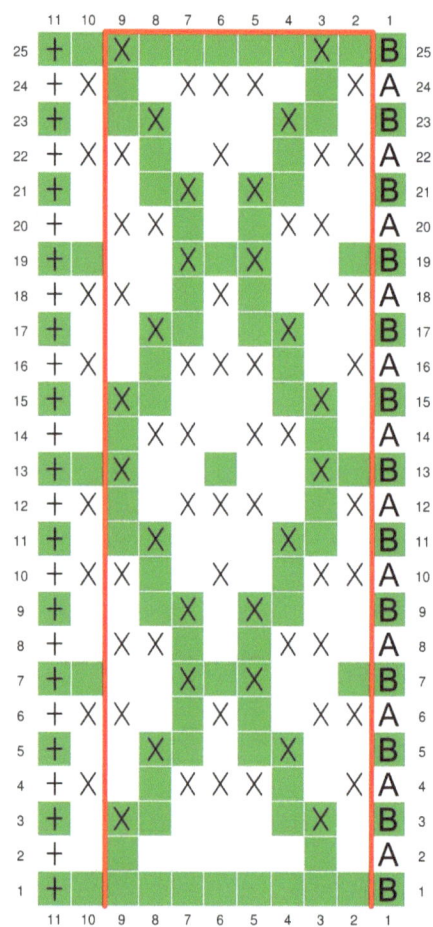

A		BBS using Color Indicated
		BLOsc
X		FLOdc
+		EBS
🟥		Repeat Across

Row 1: With Color B, BBS in 1st, BLOsc across, EBS in last.

Row 2: With Color A, BBS in 1st, BLOsc across, EBS in last.

Row 3: With Color B, BBS in 1st, *BLOsc x1,FLOdc x1, BLOsc x5, FLOdc X1*, repeat across, BLOsc x1, EBS in last.

Row 4: With Color A, BBS in 1st, *FLOdc x1, BLOsc x2, FLOdc x3, BLOsc x2*, repeat across, FLOdc x1, EBS in last.

Row 5: With Color B, BBS in 1st, *BLOsc x2, FLOdc x1, BLOsc x3, FLOdc x1, BLOsc X1*, repeat across, BLOsc x1, EBS in last.

Row 6: With Color A, BBS in 1st, *FLOdc x2, BLOsc x2, FLOdc x1, BLOsc x2, FLOdc X1*, repeat across, FLOdc x1, EBS in last.

Row 7: With Color B, BBS in 1st, *BLOsc x3, FLOdc x1, BLOsc x1,FLOdc x1, BLOsc x2*, repeat across, BLOsc x1, EBS in last.

Row 8: With Color A, BBS in 1st, *BLOsc x1,FLOdc x2, BLOsc x3, FLOdc x2*, repeat across, BLOsc x1, EBS in last.

Row 9: With Color B, BBS in 1st, *BLOsc x3, FLOdc x1, BLOsc x1,FLOdc x1, BLOsc x2*, repeat across, BLOsc x1, EBS in last.

Row 10: With Color A, BBS in 1st, *FLOdc x2, BLOsc x2, FLOdc x1, BLOsc x2, FLOdc X1*, repeat across, FLOdc x1, EBS in last.

Row 11: With Color B, BBS in 1st, *BLOsc x2, FLOdc x1, BLOsc x3, FLOdc x1, BLOsc X1*, repeat across, BLOsc x1, EBS in last.

Row 12: With Color A, BBS in 1st, *FLOdc x1, BLOsc x2, FLOdc x3, BLOsc x2*, repeat across, FLOdc x1, EBS in last.

Row 13: With Color B, BBS in 1st, *BLOsc x1,FLOdc x1, BLOsc x5, FLOdc X1*, repeat across, BLOsc x1, EBS in last.

Row 14: With Color A, BBS in 1st, *BLOsc x2, FLOdc x2, BLOsc x1,FLOdc x2, BLOsc X1*, repeat across, BLOsc x1, EBS in last.

Row 15: With Color B, BBS in 1st, *BLOsc x1,FLOdc x1, BLOsc x5, FLOdc X1*, repeat across, BLOsc x1, EBS in last.

Row 16: With Color A, BBS in 1st, *FLOdc x1, BLOsc x2, FLOdc x3, BLOsc x2*, repeat across, FLOdc x1, EBS in last.

Row 17: With Color B, BBS in 1st, *BLOsc x2, FLOdc x1, BLOsc x3, FLOdc x1, BLOsc X1*, repeat across, BLOsc x1, EBS in last.

Row 18: With Color A, BBS in 1st, *FLOdc x2, BLOsc x2, FLOdc x1, BLOsc x2, FLOdc X1*, repeat across, FLOdc x1, EBS in last.

Row 19: With Color B, BBS in 1st, *BLOsc x3, FLOdc x1, BLOsc x1,FLOdc x1, BLOsc x2*, repeat across, BLOsc x1, EBS in last.

Row 20: With Color A, BBS in 1st, *BLOsc x1,FLOdc x2, BLOsc x3, FLOdc x2*, repeat across, BLOsc x1, EBS in last.

Row 21: With Color B, BBS in 1st, *BLOsc x3, FLOdc x1, BLOsc x1,FLOdc x1, BLOsc x2*, repeat across, BLOsc x1, EBS in last.

Row 22: With Color A, BBS in 1st, *FLOdc x2, BLOsc x2, FLOdc x1, BLOsc x2, FLOdc X1*, repeat across, FLOdc x1, EBS in last.

Row 23: With Color B, BBS in 1st, *BLOsc x2, FLOdc x1, BLOsc x3, FLOdc x1, BLOsc X1*, repeat across, BLOsc x1, EBS in last.

Row 24: With Color A, BBS in 1st, *FLOdc x1, BLOsc x2, FLOdc x3, BLOsc x2*, repeat across, FLOdc x1, EBS in last.

Row 25: With Color B, BBS in 1st, *BLOsc, FLOdc, BLOsc x5, FLOdc*, repeat across, BLOsc x1, EBS in last.

Section 3-Mosaic Butterfly

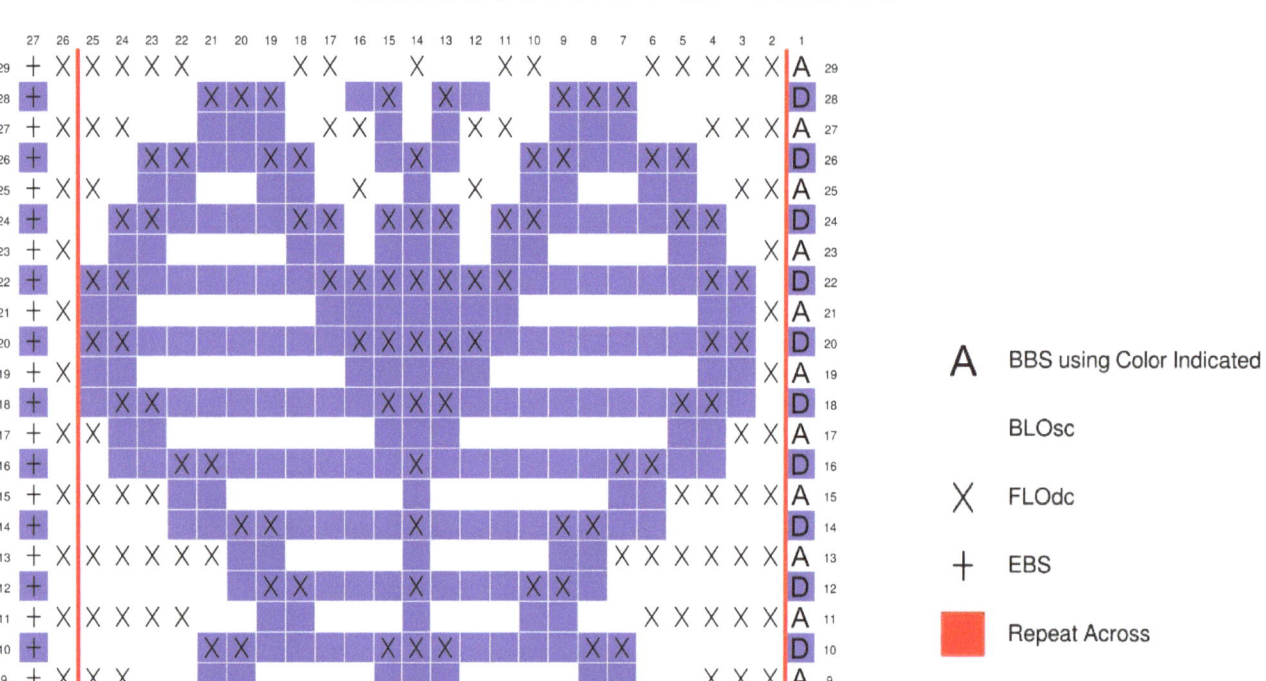

Row 1: With Color A, BBS in 1st, BLOsc across, EBS in last.

Row 2: With Color D, BBS in 1st, BLOsc across, EBS in last.

Row 3: With Color A, BBS in 1st, *FLOdc x4, BLOsc x3, FLOdc x11, BLOsc x3, FLOdc x3*, repeat across, FLOdc x1, EBS in last.

Row 4: With Color D, BBS in 1st, *BLOsc x4, FLOdc x3, BLOsc x11, FLOdc x3, BLOsc x3*, repeat across, BLOsc x1, EBS in last.

Row 5: With Color A, BBS in 1st, *FLOdc x3, BLOsc x6, FLOdc x7, BLOsc x6, FLOdc x2*, repeat across, FLOdc x1, EBS in last.

Row 6: With Color D, BBS in 1st, *BLOsc x3, FLOdc x2, BLOsc x2, FLOdc x2, BLOsc x7, FLOdc x2, BLOsc x2, FLOdc x2, BLOsc x2*, repeat across, BLOsc x1, EBS in last.

Row 7: With Color A, BBS in 1st, *FLOdc x2, BLOsc x8, FLOdc x2, BLOsc x1, FLOdc x2, BLOsc x8, FLOdc x1*, repeat across, FLOdc x1, EBS in last.

Row 8: With Color D, BBS in 1st, *BLOsc x3, FLOdc x2, BLOsc x3, FLOdc x2, BLOsc x2, FLOdc x1, BLOsc x2, FLOdc x2, BLOsc x3, FLOdc x2, BLOsc x2*, repeat across, BLOsc x1, EBS in last.

Row 9: With Color A, BBS in 1st, *FLOdc x3, BLOsc x19, FLOdc x2*, repeat across, FLOdc x1, EBS in last.

Row 10: With Color D, BBS in 1st, *BLOsc x5, FLOdc x2, BLOsc x4, FLOdc x3, BLOsc x4, FLOdc x2, BLOsc x4*, repeat across, BLOsc x1, EBS in last.

Row 11: With Color A, BBS in 1st, *FLOdc x5, BLOsc x15, FLOdc x4*, repeat across, FLOdc x1, EBS in last.

Row 12: With Color D, BBS in 1st, *BLOsc x7, FLOdc x2, BLOsc x3, FLOdc x1, BLOsc x3, FLOdc x2, BLOsc x6*, repeat across, BLOsc x1, EBS in last.

Row 13: With Color A, BBS in 1st, *FLOdc x6, BLOsc x13, FLOdc x5*, repeat across, FLOdc x1, EBS in last.

Row 14: With Color D, BBS in 1st, *BLOsc x6, FLOdc x2, BLOsc x4, FLOdc x1, BLOsc x4, FLOdc x2, BLOsc x5*, repeat across, BLOsc x1, EBS in last.

Row 15: With Color A, BBS in 1st, *FLOdc x4, BLOsc x17, FLOdc x3*, repeat across, FLOdc x1, EBS in last.

Row 16: With Color D, BBS in 1st, *BLOsc x4, FLOdc x2, BLOsc x6, FLOdc x1, BLOsc x6, FLOdc x2, BLOsc x3*, repeat across, BLOsc x1, EBS in last.

Row 17: With Color A, BBS in 1st, *FLOdc x2, BLOsc x21, FLOdc x1*, repeat across, FLOdc x1, EBS in last.

Row 18: With Color D, BBS in 1st, *BLOsc x2, FLOdc x2, BLOsc x7, FLOdc x3, BLOsc x7, FLOdc x2, BLOsc x1*, repeat across, BLOsc x1, EBS in last.

Row 19: With Color A, BBS in 1st, *FLOdc x1, BLOsc x23*, repeat across, FLOdc x1, EBS in last.

Row 20: With Color D, BBS in 1st, *BLOsc x1, FLOdc x2, BLOsc x7, FLOdc x5, BLOsc x7, FLOdc x2*, repeat across, BLOsc x1, EBS in last.

Row 21: With Color A, BBS in 1st, *FLOdc x1, BLOsc x23*, repeat across, FLOdc x1, EBS in last.

Row 22: With Color D, BBS in 1st, *BLOsc x1, FLOdc x2, BLOsc x6, FLOdc x7, BLOsc x6, FLOdc x2*, repeat across, BLOsc x1, EBS in last.

Row 23: With Color A, BBS in 1st, *FLOdc x1, BLOsc x23*, repeat across, FLOdc x1, EBS in last.

Row 24: With Color D, BBS in 1st, *BLOsc x2, FLOdc x2, BLOsc x4, FLOdc x2, BLOsc x1, FLOdc x3, BLOsc x1, FLOdc x2, BLOsc x4, FLOdc x2, BLOsc x1*, repeat across, BLOsc x1, EBS in last.

Row 25: With Color A, BBS in 1st, *FLOdc x2, BLOsc x8, FLOdc x1, BLOsc x3, FLOdc x1, BLOsc x8, FLOdc x1*, repeat across, FLOdc x1, EBS in last.

24

Section 3-Mosaic Butterfly

Row 26: With Color D, BBS in 1st, *BLOsc x3, FLOdc x2, BLOsc x2, FLOdc x2, BLOsc x3, FLOdc x1, BLOsc x3, FLOdc x2, BLOsc x2, FLOdc x2, BLOsc x2*, repeat across, BLOsc x1, EBS in last.

Row 27: With Color A, BBS in 1st, *FLOdc x3, BLOsc x6, FLOdc x2, BLOsc x3, FLOdc x2, BLOsc x6, FLOdc x2*, repeat across, FLOdc x1, EBS in last.

Row 28: With Color D, BBS in 1st, *BLOsc x5, FLOdc x3, BLOsc x3, FLOdc x1, BLOsc x1, FLOdc x1, BLOsc x3, FLOdc x3, BLOsc x4*, repeat across, BLOsc x1, EBS in last.

Row 29: With Color A, BBS in 1st, *FLOdc x5, BLOsc x3, FLOdc x2, BLOsc x2, FLOdc x1, BLOsc x2, FLOdc x2, BLOsc x3, FLOdc x4*, repeat across, FLOdc x1, EBS in last.

Mosaic Flower Garden

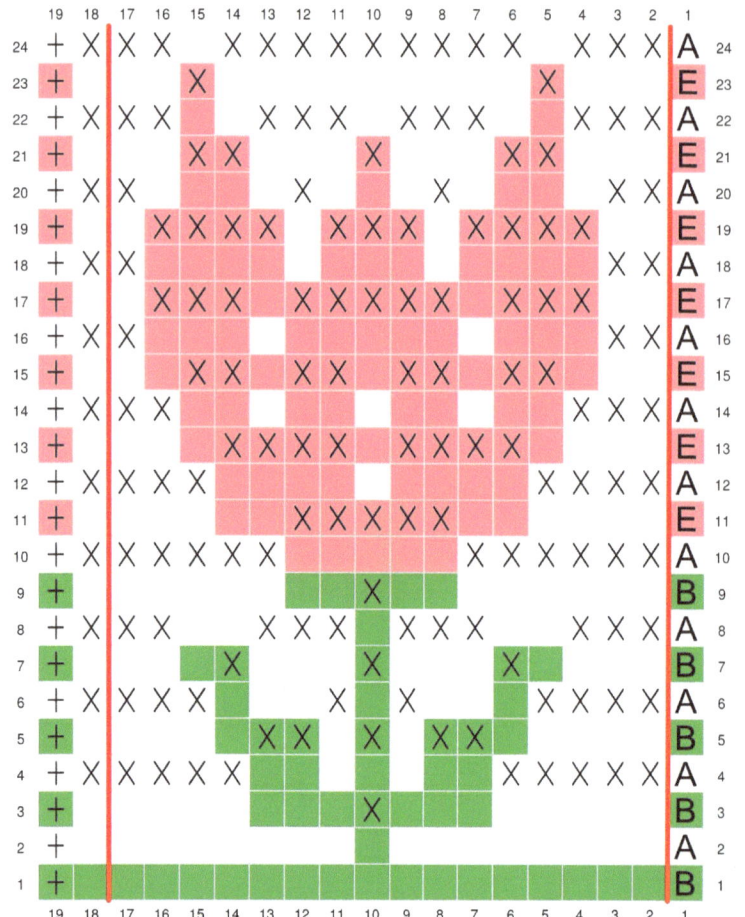

A	BBS using Color Indicated
	BLOsc
X	FLOdc
+	EBS
🟥	Repeat Across

Row 1: With Color B, BS in 1st, BLOsc across, EBS in last.

Row 2: BS in 1st, BLOsc across, EBS in last.

Row 3: With Color B, BBS in 1st, *BLOsc x8, FLOdc x1, BLOsc x7*, repeat across, BLOsc x1, EBS in last.

Row 4: With Color A, BBS in 1st, *FLOdc x5, BLOsc x7, FLOdc x4*, repeat across, FLOdc x1, EBS in last.

Bow 5: With Color B, BBS in 1st, *BLOsc x5, FLOdc x2, BLOsc x1, FLOdc x1, BLOsc x1, FLOdc x2, BLOsc x4*, repeat across, BLOsc x1, EBS in last.

Row 6: With Color A, BBS in 1st, *FLOdc x4, BLOsc x3, FLOdc x1, BLOsc x1, FLOdc x1, BLOsc x3, FLOdc x3*, repeat across, FLOdc x1, EBS in last.

Row 7: With Color B, BBS in 1st, *BLOsc x4, FLOdc x1, BLOsc x3, FLOdc x1, BLOsc x3, FLOdc x1, BLOsc x3*, repeat across, BLOsc x1, EBS in last.

Row 8: With Color A, BBS in 1st, *FLOdc x3, BLOsc x2, FLOdc x3, BLOsc x1, FLOdc x3, BLOsc x2, FLOdc x2*, repeat across, FLOdc x1, EBS in last.

Row 9: With Color B, BBS in 1st, *BLOsc x8, FLOdc x1, BLOsc x7*, repeat across, BLOsc x1, EBS in last.

Row 10: With Color A, BBS in 1st, *FLOdc x6, BLOsc x5, FLOdc x5*, repeat across, FLOdc x1, EBS in last.

Row 11: With Color E, BBS in 1st, *BLOsc x6, FLOdc x5, BLOsc x5*, repeat across, BLOsc x1, EBS in last.

Row 12: With Color A, BBS in 1st, *FLOdc x4, BLOsc x9, FLOdc x3*, repeat across, FLOdc x1, EBS in last.

Row 13: With Color E, BBS in 1st, *BLOsc x4, FLOdc x4, BLOsc x1, FLOdc x4, BLOsc x3*, repeat across, BLOsc x1, EBS in last.

Row 14: With Color A, BBS in 1st, *FLOdc x3, BLOsc x11, FLOdc x2*, repeat across, FLOdc x1, EBS in last.

Row 15: With Color E, BBS in 1st, *BLOsc x3, FLOdc x2, BLOsc x1, FLOdc x2, BLOsc x1, FLOdc x2, BLOsc x1, FLOdc x2, BLOsc x2*, repeat across, BLOsc x1, EBS in last.

Row 16: With Color A, BBS in 1st, *FLOdc x2, BLOsc x13, FLOdc x1*, repeat across, FLOdc x1, EBS in last.

Row 17: With Color E, BBS in 1st, *BLOsc x2, FLOdc x3, BLOsc x1, FLOdc x5, BLOsc x1, FLOdc x3, BLOsc x1*, repeat across, BLOsc x1, EBS in last.

Row 18: With Color A, BBS in 1st, *FLOdc x2, BLOsc x13, FLOdc x1*, repeat across, FLOdc x1, EBS in last.

Row 19: With Color E, BBS in 1st, *BLOsc x2, FLOdc x4, BLOsc x1, FLOdc x3, BLOsc x1, FLOdc x4, BLOsc x1*, repeat across, BLOsc x1, EBS in last.

Row 20: With Color A, BBS in 1st, *FLOdc x2, BLOsc x4, FLOdc x1, BLOsc x3, FLOdc x1, BLOsc x4, FLOdc x1*, repeat across, FLOdc x1, EBS in last.

Row 21: With Color E, BBS in 1st, *BLOsc x3, FLOdc x2, BLOsc x3, FLOdc x1, BLOsc x3, FLOdc x2, BLOsc x2*, repeat across, BLOsc x1, EBS in last.

Row 22: With Color A, BBS in 1st, *FLOdc x3, BLOsc x2, FLOdc x3, BLOsc x1, FLOdc x3, BLOsc x2, FLOdc x2*, repeat across, FLOdc x1, EBS in last.

Row 23: With Color E, BBS in 1st, *BLOsc x3, FLOdc x1, BLOsc x9, FLOdc x1, BLOsc x2*, repeat across, BLOsc x1, EBS in last.

Row 24: With Color A, BBS in 1st, *FLOdc x3, BLOsc x1, FLOdc x9, BLOsc x1, FLOdc x2*, repeat across, FLOdc x1, EBS in last.

Section 5-Lovely Lattice

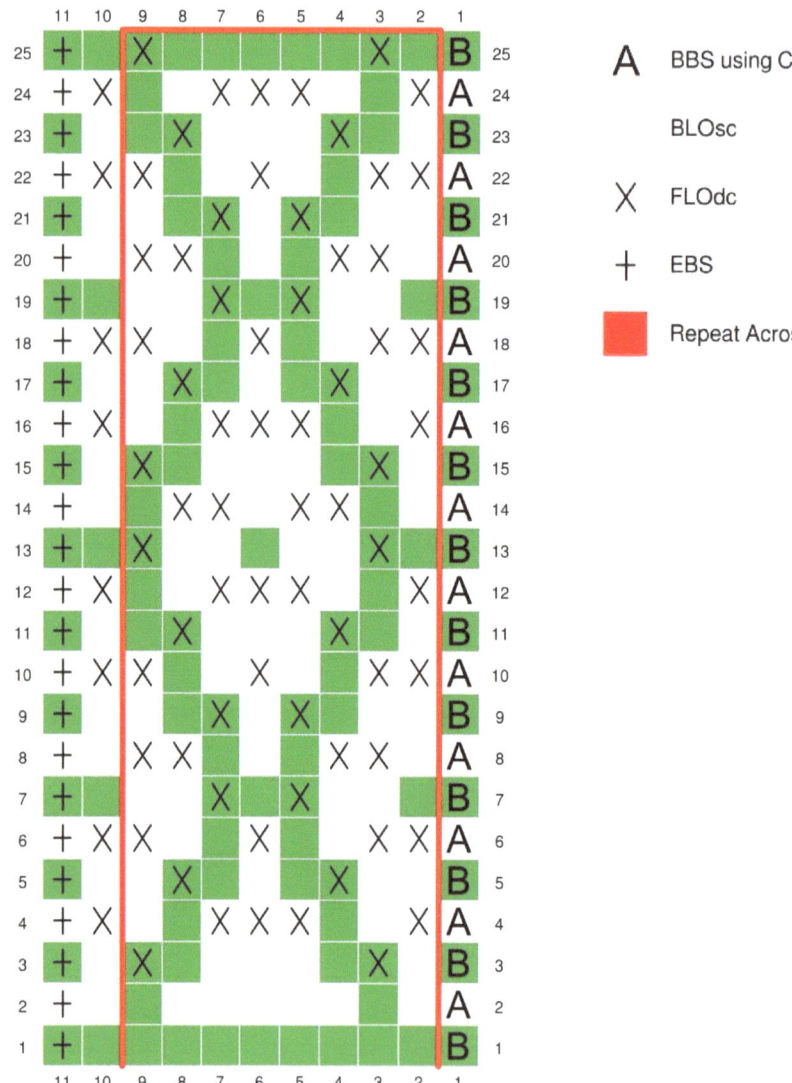

		Legend
A		BBS using Color Indicated
		BLOsc
X		FLOdc
+		EBS
■		Repeat Across

Row 1: With Color B, BBS in 1st, BLOsc across, EBS in last.

Row 2: With Color A, BBS in 1st, BLOsc across, EBS in last.

Row 3: With Color B, BBS in 1st, *BLOsc x1,FLOdc x1, BLOsc x5, FLOdc X1*, repeat across, BLOsc x1, EBS in last.

Row 4: With Color A, BBS in 1st, *FLOdc x1, BLOsc x2, FLOdc x3, BLOsc x2*, repeat across, FLOdc x1, EBS in last.

Row 5: With Color B, BBS in 1st, *BLOsc x2, FLOdc x1, BLOsc x3, FLOdc x1, BLOsc X1*, repeat across, BLOsc x1, EBS in last.

Row 6: With Color A, BBS in 1st, *FLOdc x2, BLOsc x2, FLOdc x1, BLOsc x2, FLOdc X1*, repeat across, FLOdc x1, EBS in last.

Row 7: With Color B, BBS in 1st, *BLOsc x3, FLOdc x1, BLOsc x1,FLOdc x1, BLOsc x2*, repeat across, BLOsc x1, EBS in last.

Row 8: With Color A, BBS in 1st, *BLOsc x1,FLOdc x2, BLOsc x3, FLOdc x2*, repeat across, BLOsc x1, EBS in last

Row 9: With Color B, BBS in 1st, *BLOsc x3, FLOdc x1, BLOsc x1,FLOdc x1, BLOsc x2*, repeat across, BLOsc x1, EBS in last.

Row 10: With Color A, BBS in 1st, *FLOdc x2, BLOsc x2, FLOdc x1, BLOsc x2, FLOdc X1*, repeat across, FLOdc x1, EBS in last.

Row 11: With Color B, BBS in 1st, *BLOsc x2, FLOdc x1, BLOsc x3, FLOdc x1, BLOsc X1*, repeat across, BLOsc x1, EBS in last.

Row 12: With Color A, BBS in 1st, *FLOdc x1, BLOsc x2, FLOdc x3, BLOsc x2*, repeat across, FLOdc x1, EBS in last.

Row 13: With Color B, BBS in 1st, *BLOsc x1,FLOdc x1, BLOsc x5, FLOdc X1*, repeat across, BLOsc x1, EBS in last.

Row 14: With Color A, BBS in 1st, *BLOsc x2, FLOdc x2, BLOsc x1,FLOdc x2, BLOsc X1*, repeat across, BLOsc x1, EBS in last.

Row 15: With Color B, BBS in 1st, *BLOsc x1,FLOdc x1, BLOsc x5, FLOdc X1*, repeat across, BLOsc x1, EBS in last.

Row 16: With Color A, BBS in 1st, *FLOdc x1, BLOsc x2, FLOdc x3, BLOsc x2*, repeat across, FLOdc x1, EBS in last.

Row 17: With Color B, BBS in 1st, *BLOsc x2, FLOdc x1, BLOsc x3, FLOdc x1, BLOsc X1*, repeat across, BLOsc x1, EBS in last.

Row 18: With Color A, BBS in 1st, *FLOdc x2, BLOsc x2, FLOdc x1, BLOsc x2, FLOdc X1*, repeat across, FLOdc x1, EBS in last.

Row 19: With Color B, BBS in 1st, *BLOsc x3, FLOdc x1, BLOsc x1,FLOdc x1, BLOsc x2*, repeat across, BLOsc x1, EBS in last.

Row 20: With Color A, BBS in 1st, *BLOsc x1,FLOdc x2, BLOsc x3, FLOdc x2*, repeat across, BLOsc x1, EBS in last.

Row 21: With Color B, BBS in 1st, *BLOsc x3, FLOdc x1, BLOsc x1,FLOdc x1, BLOsc x2*, repeat across, BLOsc x1, EBS in last.

Row 22: With Color A, BBS in 1st, *FLOdc x2, BLOsc x2, FLOdc x1, BLOsc x2, FLOdc X1*, repeat across, FLOdc x1, EBS in last.

Row 23: With Color B, BBS in 1st, *BLOsc x2, FLOdc x1, BLOsc x3, FLOdc x1, BLOsc X1*, repeat across, BLOsc x1, EBS in last.

Row 24: With Color A, BBS in 1st, *FLOdc x1, BLOsc x2, FLOdc x3, BLOsc x2*, repeat across, FLOdc x1, EBS in last.

Row 25: With Color B, BBS in 1st, *BLOsc, FLOdc, BLOsc x5, FLOdc*, repeat across, BLOsc x1, EBS in last.

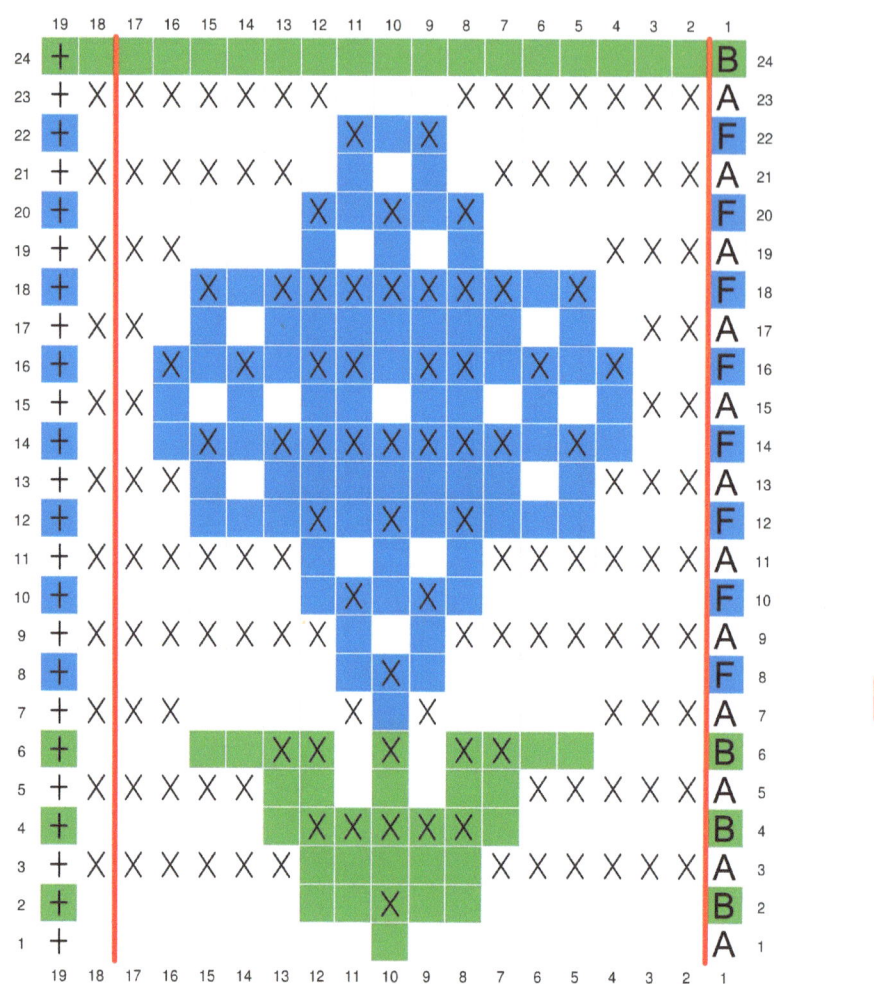

Legend:

A — BBS using Color Indicated

BLOsc

X — FLOdc

+ — EBS

🟥 Repeat Across

Row 1: With Color A, BBS in 1st, BLOsc across, EBS in last.

Row 2: With Color B, BBS in 1st, *BLOsc x8, FLOdc x1, BLOsc x7*, repeat across, BLOsc x1, EBS in last.

Row 3: With Color A, BBS in 1st, *FLOdc x6, BLOsc x5, FLOdc x5*, repeat across, FLOdc x1, EBS in last.

Row 4: With Color B, BBS in 1st, *BLOsc x6, FLOdc x5, BLOsc x5*, repeat across, BLOsc x1, EBS in last.

Row 5: With Color A, BBS in 1st, *FLOdc x5, BLOsc x7, FLOdc x4*, repeat across, FLOdc x1, EBS in last.

Row 6: With Color B, BBS in 1st, *BLOsc x5, FLOdc x2, BLOsc x1, FLOdc x1, BLOsc x1, FLOdc x2, BLOsc x4*, repeat across, BLOsc x1, EBS in last.

Row 7: With Color A, BBS in 1st, *FLOdc x3, BLOsc x4, FLOdc x1, BLOsc x1, FLOdc x1, BLOsc x4, FLOdc x2*, repeat across, FLOdc x1, EBS in last.

Row 8: With Color F, BBS in 1st, *BLOsc x8, FLOdc x1, BLOsc x7*, repeat across, BLOsc x1, EBS in last.

Row 9: With Color A, BBS in 1st, *FLOdc x7, BLOsc x3, FLOdc x6*, repeat across, FLOdc x1, EBS in last.

Row 10: With Color F, BBS in 1st, *BLOsc x7, FLOdc x1, BLOsc x1, FLOdc x1, BLOsc x6*, repeat across, BLOsc x1, EBS in last.

Row 11: With Color A, BBS in 1st, *FLOdc x6, BLOsc x5, FLOdc x5*, repeat across, FLOdc x1, EBS in last.

Row 12: With Color F, BBS in 1st, *BLOsc x6, FLOdc x1, BLOsc x1, FLOdc x1, BLOsc x1, FLOdc x1, BLOsc x5*, repeat across, BLOsc x1, EBS in last.

Row 13: With Color A, BBS in 1st, *FLOdc x3, BLOsc x11, FLOdc x2*, repeat across, FLOdc x1, EBS in last.

Row 14: With Color F, BBS in 1st, *BLOsc x3, FLOdc x1, BLOsc x1, FLOdc x7, BLOsc x1, FLOdc x1, BLOsc x2*, repeat across, BLOsc x1, EBS in last.

Mosaic Flower Garden

Row 15: With Color A, BBS in 1st, *FLOdc x2, BLOsc x13, FLOdc x1*, repeat across, FLOdc x1, EBS in last.

Row 16: With Color F, BBS in 1st, *BLOsc x2, FLOdc x1, BLOsc x1, FLOdc x1, BLOsc x1, FLOdc x2, BLOsc x1, FLOdc x2, BLOsc x1, FLOdc x1, BLOsc x1, FLOdc x1, BLOsc x1*, repeat across, BLOsc x1, EBS in last.

Row 17: With Color A, BBS in 1st, *FLOdc x2, BLOsc x13, FLOdc x1*, repeat across, FLOdc x1, EBS in last.

Row 18: With Color F, BBS in 1st, *BLOsc x3, FLOdc x1, BLOsc x1, FLOdc x7, BLOsc x1, FLOdc x1, BLOsc x2*, repeat across, BLOsc x1, EBS in last.

Row 19: With Color A, BBS in 1st, *FLOdc x3, BLOsc x11, FLOdc x2*, repeat across, FLOdc x1, EBS in last.

Row 20: With Color F, BBS in 1st, *BLOsc x6, FLOdc x1, BLOsc x1, FLOdc x1, BLOsc x1, FLOdc x1, BLOsc x5*, repeat across, BLOsc x1, EBS in last.

Row 21: With Color A, BBS in 1st, *FLOdc x6, BLOsc x5, FLOdc x5*, repeat across, FLOdc x1, EBS in last.

Row 22: With Color F, BBS in 1st, *BLOsc x7, FLOdc x1, BLOsc x1, FLOdc x1, BLOsc x6*, repeat across, BLOsc x1, EBS in last.

Row 23: With Color A, BBS in 1st, *FLOdc x7, BLOsc x3, FLOdc x6*, repeat across, FLOdc x1, EBS in last.

Row 24: With Color B, BBS in 1st, BLOsc across, EBS in last.

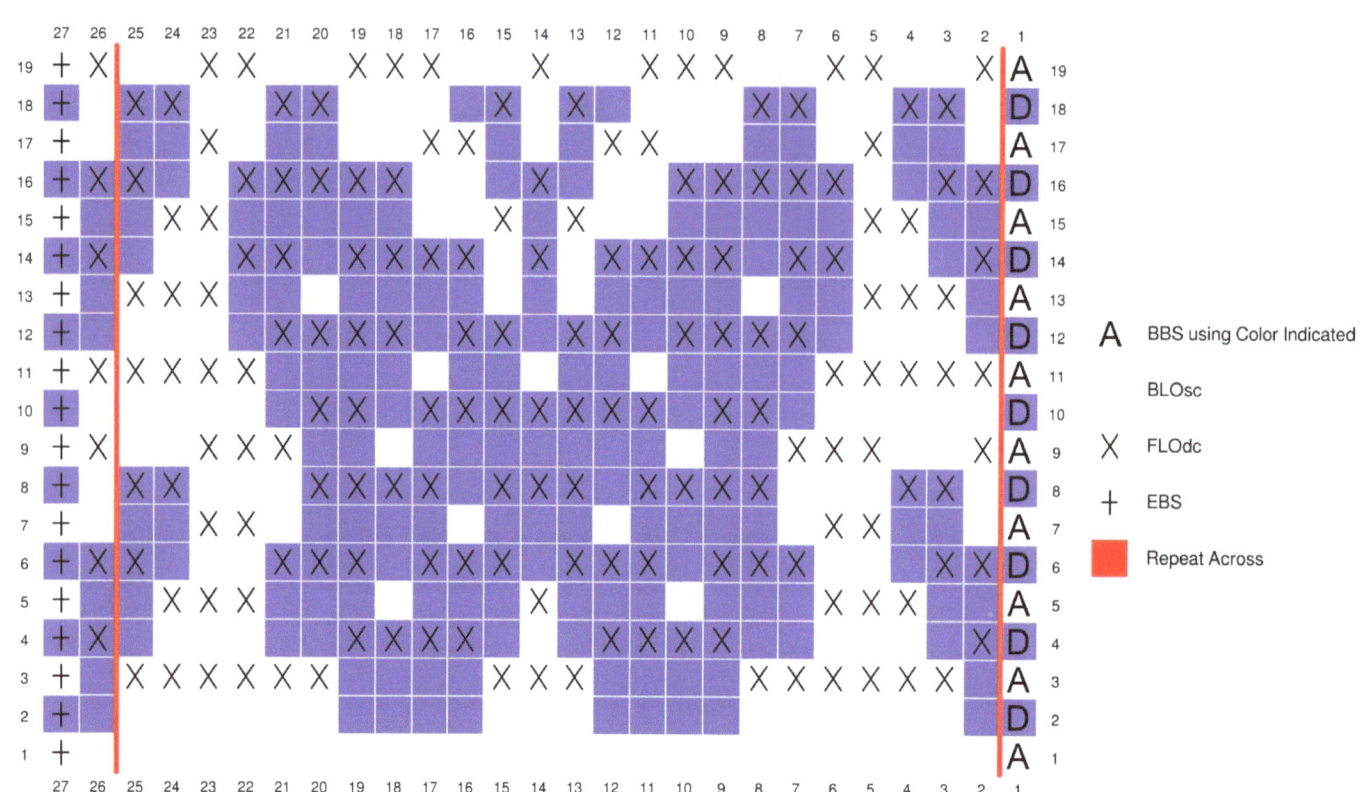

Row 1: With Color A, BBS in 1st, BLOsc across, EBS in last.

Row 2: With Color D, BBS in 1st, BLOsc across, EBS in last.

Row 3: With Color A, BBS in 1st, *BLOsc x1, FLOdc x6, BLOsc x4, FLOdc x3, BLOsc x4, FLOdc x6*, repeat across, BLOsc x1, EBS in last.

Row 4: With Color D, BBS in 1st, *FLOdc x1, BLOsc x6, FLOdc x4, BLOsc x3, FLOdc x4, BLOsc x6*, repeat across, FLOdc x1, EBS in last.

Row 5: With Color A, BBS in 1st, *BLOsc x2, FLOdc x3, BLOsc x7, FLOdc x1, BLOsc x7, FLOdc x3, BLOsc x1*, repeat across, BLOsc x1, EBS in last.

Row 6: With Color D, BBS in 1st, *FLOdc x2, BLOsc x3, FLOdc x3, BLOsc x1, FLOdc x3, BLOsc x1, FLOdc x3, BLOsc x1, FLOdc x3, BLOsc x3, FLOdc x1*, repeat across, FLOdc x1, EBS in last.

Row 7: With Color A, BBS in 1st, *BLOsc x3, FLOdc x2, BLOsc x15, FLOdc x2, BLOsc x2*, repeat across, BLOsc x1, EBS in last.

Row 8: With Color D, BBS in 1st, *BLOsc x1, FLOdc x2, BLOsc x3, FLOdc x4, BLOsc x1, FLOdc x3, BLOsc x1, FLOdc x4, BLOsc x3, FLOdc x2*, repeat across, BLOsc x1, EBS in last.

Row 9: With Color A, BBS in 1st, *FLOdc x1, BLOsc x2, FLOdc x3, BLOsc x13, FLOdc x3, BLOsc x2*, repeat across, FLOdc x1, EBS in last.

Row 10: With Color D, BBS in 1st, *BLOsc x6, FLOdc x2, BLOsc x1, FLOdc x7, BLOsc x1, FLOdc x2, BLOsc x5*, repeat across, BLOsc x1, EBS in last.

Row 11: With Color A, BBS in 1st, *FLOdc x5, BLOsc x15, FLOdc x4*, repeat across, FLOdc x1, EBS in last.

Row 12: With Color D, BBS in 1st, *BLOsc x5, FLOdc x4, BLOsc x1, FLOdc x2, BLOsc x1, FLOdc x2, BLOsc x1, FLOdc x4, BLOsc x4*, repeat across, BLOsc x1, EBS in last.

Row 13: With Color A, BBS in 1st, *BLOsc x1, FLOdc x3, BLOsc x17, FLOdc x3*, repeat across, BLOsc x1, EBS in last.

Row 14: With Color D, BBS in 1st, *FLOdc x1, BLOsc x3, FLOdc x2, BLOsc x1, FLOdc x4, BLOsc x1, FLOdc x1, BLOsc x1, FLOdc x4, BLOsc x1, FLOdc x2, BLOsc x3*, repeat across, FLOdc x1, EBS in last.

Row 15: With Color A, BBS in 1st, *BLOsc x2, FLOdc x2, BLOsc x7, FLOdc x1, BLOsc x1, FLOdc x1, BLOsc x7, FLOdc x2, BLOsc x1*, repeat across, BLOsc x1, EBS in last.

Section 7-Small Butterfly & Heart

Row 16: With Color D, BBS in 1st, *FLOdc x2, BLOsc x2, FLOdc x5, BLOsc x3, FLOdc x1, BLOsc x3, FLOdc x5, BLOsc x2, FLOdc x1*, repeat across, FLOdc x1, EBS in last.

Row 17: With Color A, BBS in 1st, *BLOsc x3, FLOdc x1, BLOsc x5, FLOdc x2, BLOsc x3, FLOdc x2, BLOsc x5, FLOdc x1, BLOsc x2*, repeat across, BLOsc x1, EBS in last.

Row 18: With Color D, BBS in 1st, *BLOsc x1, FLOdc x2, BLOsc x2, FLOdc x2, BLOsc x4, FLOdc x1, BLOsc x1, FLOdc x1, BLOsc x4, FLOdc x2, BLOsc x2, FLOdc x2*, repeat across, BLOsc x1, EBS in last.

Row 19: With Color A, BBS in 1st, *FLOdc x1, BLOsc x2, FLOdc x2, BLOsc x2, FLOdc x3, BLOsc x2, FLOdc x1, BLOsc x2, FLOdc x3, BLOsc x2, FLOdc x2, BLOsc x2*, repeat across, FLOdc x1, EBS in last.

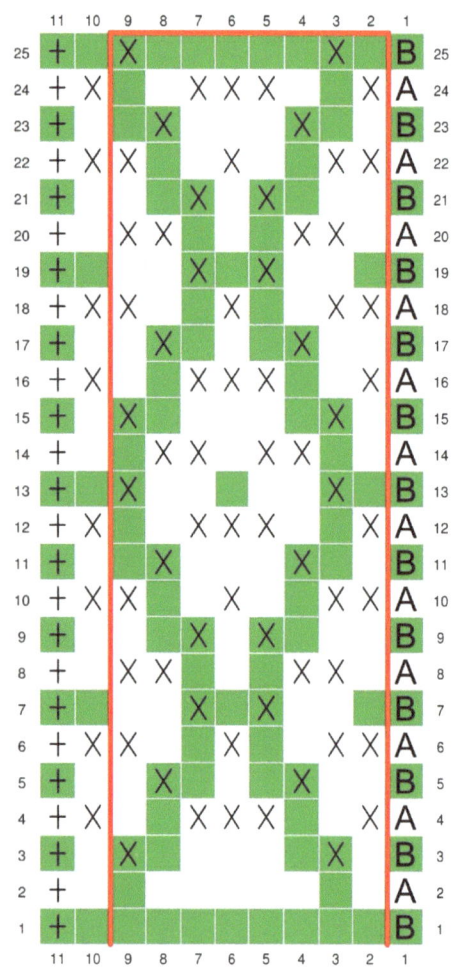

	A	BBS using Color Indicated
		BLOsc
	X	FLOdc
	+	EBS
	▮	Repeat Across

Row 1: With Color B, BBS in 1st, BLOsc across, EBS in last.

Row 2: With Color A, BBS in 1st, BLOsc across, EBS in last.

Row 3: With Color B, BBS in 1st, *BLOsc x1,FLOdc x1, BLOsc x5, FLOdc X1*, repeat across, BLOsc x1, EBS in last.

Row 4: With Color A, BBS in 1st, *FLOdc x1, BLOsc x2, FLOdc x3, BLOsc x2*, repeat across, FLOdc x1, EBS in last.

Row 5: With Color B, BBS in 1st, *BLOsc x2, FLOdc x1, BLOsc x3, FLOdc x1, BLOsc X1*, repeat across, BLOsc x1, EBS in last.

Row 6: With Color A, BBS in 1st, *FLOdc x2, BLOsc x2, FLOdc x1, BLOsc x2, FLOdc X1*, repeat across, FLOdc x1, EBS in last.

Row 7: With Color B, BBS in 1st, *BLOsc x3, FLOdc x1, BLOsc x1,FLOdc x1, BLOsc x2*, repeat across, BLOsc x1, EBS in last.

Row 8: With Color A, BBS in 1st, *BLOsc x1,FLOdc x2, BLOsc x3, FLOdc x2*, repeat across, BLOsc x1, EBS in last.

Row 9: With Color B, BBS in 1st, *BLOsc x3, FLOdc x1, BLOsc x1,FLOdc x1, BLOsc x2*, repeat across, BLOsc x1, EBS in last.

Row 10: With Color A, BBS in 1st, *FLOdc x2, BLOsc x2, FLOdc x1, BLOsc x2, FLOdc X1*, repeat across, FLOdc x1, EBS in last.

Row 11: With Color B, BBS in 1st, *BLOsc x2, FLOdc x1, BLOsc x3, FLOdc x1, BLOsc X1*, repeat across, BLOsc x1, EBS in last.

Row 12: With Color A, BBS in 1st, *FLOdc x1, BLOsc x2, FLOdc x3, BLOsc x2*, repeat across, FLOdc x1, EBS in last.

Row 13: With Color B, BBS in 1st, *BLOsc x1,FLOdc x1, BLOsc x5, FLOdc X1*, repeat across, BLOsc x1, EBS in last.

Row 14: With Color A, BBS in 1st, *BLOsc x2, FLOdc x2, BLOsc x1,FLOdc x2, BLOsc X1*, repeat across, BLOsc x1, EBS in last.

Row 15: With Color B, BBS in 1st, *BLOsc x1,FLOdc x1, BLOsc x5, FLOdc X1*, repeat across, BLOsc x1, EBS in last.

Mosaic Flower Garden

Row 16: With Color A, BBS in 1st, *FLOdc x1, BLOsc x2, FLOdc x3, BLOsc x2*, repeat across, FLOdc x1, EBS in last.

Row 17: With Color B, BBS in 1st, *BLOsc x2, FLOdc x1, BLOsc x3, FLOdc x1, BLOsc X1*, repeat across, BLOsc x1, EBS in last.

Row 18: With Color A, BBS in 1st, *FLOdc x2, BLOsc x2, FLOdc x1, BLOsc x2, FLOdc X1*, repeat across, FLOdc x1, EBS in last.

Row 19: With Color B, BBS in 1st, *BLOsc x3, FLOdc x1, BLOsc x1,FLOdc x1, BLOsc x2*, repeat across, BLOsc x1, EBS in last.

Row 20: With Color A, BBS in 1st, *BLOsc x1,FLOdc x2, BLOsc x3, FLOdc x2*, repeat across, BLOsc x1, EBS in last.

Row 21: With Color B, BBS in 1st, *BLOsc x3, FLOdc x1, BLOsc x1,FLOdc x1, BLOsc x2*, repeat across, BLOsc x1, EBS in last.

Row 22: With Color A, BBS in 1st, *FLOdc x2, BLOsc x2, FLOdc x1, BLOsc x2, FLOdc X1*, repeat across, FLOdc x1, EBS in last.

Row 23: With Color B, BBS in 1st, *BLOsc x2, FLOdc x1, BLOsc x3, FLOdc x1, BLOsc X1*, repeat across, BLOsc x1, EBS in last.

Row 24: With Color A, BBS in 1st, *FLOdc x1, BLOsc x2, FLOdc x3, BLOsc x2*, repeat across, FLOdc x1, EBS in last.

Row 25: With Color B, BBS in 1st, *BLOsc, FLOdc, BLOsc x5, FLOdc*, repeat across, BLOsc x1, EBS in last.

Legend:

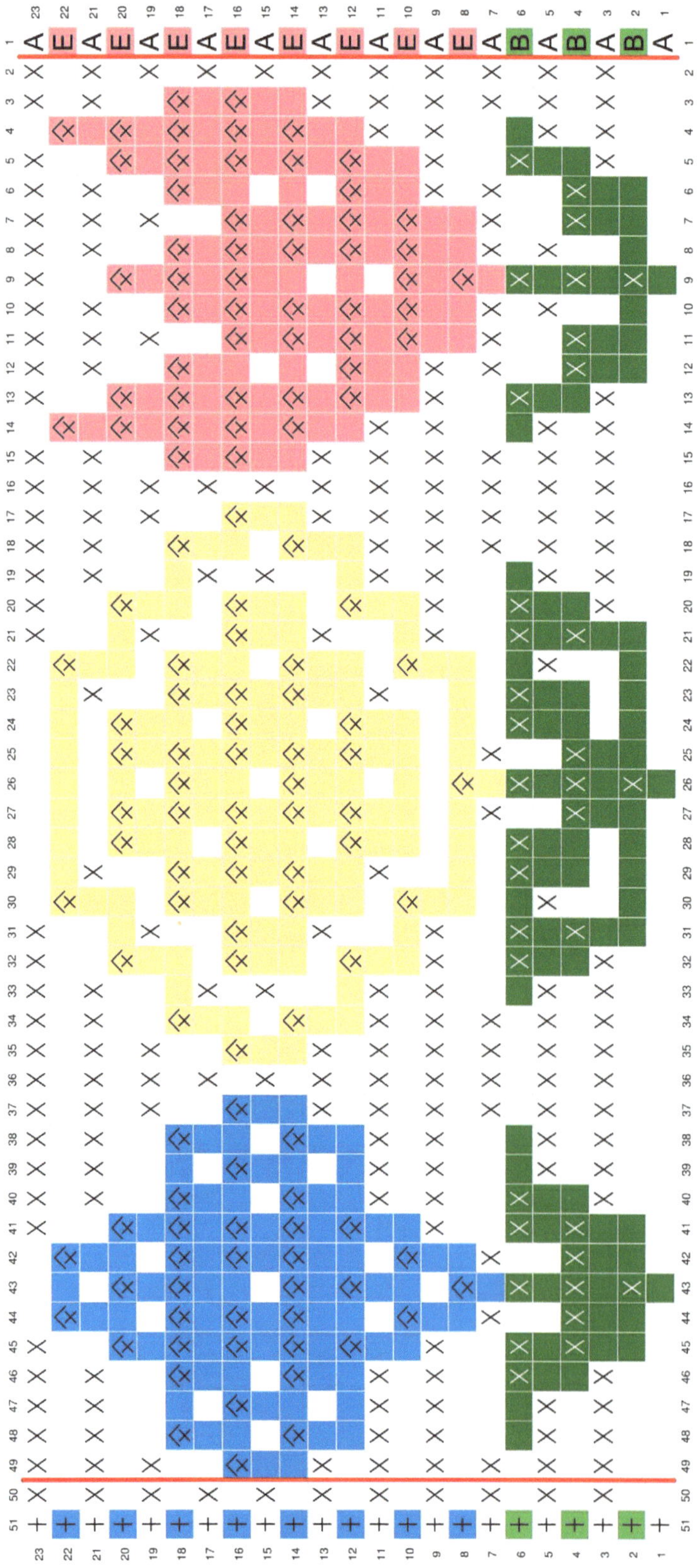

A — BBS using Color Indicated

— BLOsc

X — FLOdc

⟨X⟩ — Anc-FLOdc

+ — EBS

■ — Repeat Across

Video tutorial for color changes beginning in Row 8.

Row 1: With Color A, BBS in 1st, BLOsc across, EBS in last.

Row 2: With Color B, BBS in 1st, *BLOsc x7, FLOdc x1, BLOsc x16, FLOdc x1, BLOsc x16, FLOdc x1, BLOsc x6*, repeat across, BLOsc x1, EBS in last.

Row 3: With Color A, BBS in 1st, *FLOdc x4, BLOsc x7, FLOdc x8, BLOsc x11, FLOdc x9, BLOsc x5, FLOdc x4*, repeat across, FLOdc x1, EBS in last.

Row 4: With Color B, BBS in 1st, *BLOsc x4, FLOdc x2, BLOsc x1, FLOdc x1, BLOsc x1, FLOdc x2, BLOsc x8, FLOdc x1, BLOsc x3, FLOdc x3, BLOsc x3, FLOdc x1, BLOsc x9, FLOdc x5, BLOsc x4*, repeat across, BLOsc x1, EBS in last.

Row 5: With Color A, BBS in 1st, *FLOdc x3, BLOsc x3, FLOdc x1, BLOsc x1, FLOdc x1, BLOsc x3, FLOdc x6, BLOsc x2, FLOdc x1, BLOsc x7, FLOdc x1, BLOsc x2, FLOdc x7, BLOsc x7, FLOdc x3*, repeat across, FLOdc x1, EBS in last.

Row 6: With Color B, BBS in 1st, *BLOsc x3, FLOdc x1, BLOsc x3, FLOdc x1, BLOsc x3, FLOdc x1, BLOsc x6, FLOdc x2, BLOsc x1, FLOdc x2, BLOsc x1, FLOdc x1, BLOsc x1, FLOdc x2, BLOsc x1, FLOdc x2, BLOsc x7, FLOdc x2, BLOsc x1, FLOdc x1, BLOsc x1, FLOdc x2, BLOsc x3*, repeat across, BLOsc x1, EBS in last.

Row 7: With Color A, BBS in 1st, *FLOdc x2, BLOsc x2, FLOdc x3, BLOsc x1, FLOdc x3, BLOsc x2, FLOdc x4, BLOsc x6, FLOdc x1, BLOsc x1, FLOdc x1, BLOsc x6, FLOdc x4, BLOsc x4, FLOdc x1, BLOsc x1, FLOdc x1, BLOsc x4, FLOdc x1*, repeat across, FLOdc x1, EBS in last.

*Row 8: With Color E and *carrying* Colors C & F, BBS in 1st, *BLOsc x7, Anc-FLOdc x1, BLOsc x7, change to Color C, BLOsc x9, Anc-FLOdc x1, BLOsc x10, change to Color F, BLOsc x6, Anc-FLOdc x1, BLOsc x6*, repeat, BLOsc x1, EBS in last.

*Pay extra attention to these rows for the color change.

Section 9-Flower Garden

Row 9: With Color A, BBS in 1st, *FLOdc x5, BLOsc x5, FLOdc x10, BLOsc x9, FLOdc x11, BLOsc x3, FLOdc x5*, repeat across, FLOdc x1, EBS in last.

*Row 10: With Color E and *carrying* Colors C & F, BBS in 1st, *BLOsc x5, Anc-FLOdc x5, BLOsc x5, change to Color C, BLOsc x5, Anc-FLOdc x1, BLOsc x7, Anc-FLOdc x1, BLOsc x6, change to Color F, BLOsc x5, Anc-FLOdc x1, BLOsc x1, Anc-FLOdc x1, BLOsc x5*, repeat across, BLOsc x1, EBS in last.

Row 11: With Color A, BBS in 1st, *FLOdc x3, BLOsc x9, FLOdc x6, BLOsc x3, FLOdc x1, BLOsc x5, FLOdc x1, BLOsc x3, FLOdc x8, BLOsc x5, FLOdc x4*, repeat across, FLOdc x1, EBS in last.

*Row 12: With Color E and carrying Colors C & F, BBS in 1st, *BLOsc x3, Anc-FLOdc x4, BLOsc x1, Anc-FLOdc x4, BLOsc x3, change to Color C, BLOsc x3, Anc-FLOdc x1, BLOsc x3, Anc-FLOdc x2, BLOsc x1, Anc-FLOdc x2, BLOsc x3, Anc-FLOdc x1, BLOsc x4, change to Color F, BLOsc x4, Anc-FLOdc x1, BLOsc x1, Anc-FLOdc x1, BLOsc x1, Anc-FLOdc x1, BLOsc x4*, repeat across, BLOsc x1, EBS in last.

Row 13: With Color A, BBS in 1st, *FLOdc x2, BLOsc x11, FLOdc x3, BLOsc x3, FLOdc x1, BLOsc x9, FLOdc x1, BLOsc x3, FLOdc x3, BLOsc x11, FLOdc x1*, repeat across, FLOdc x1, EBS in last.

*Row 14: With Color E and carrying Colors C & F, BBS in 1st, *BLOsc x2, Anc-FLOdc x2, BLOsc x1, Anc-FLOdc x2, BLOsc x1, Anc-FLOdc x2, BLOsc x1, Anc-FLOdc x2, BLOsc x2, change to Color C, BLOsc x1, Anc-FLOdc x1, BLOsc x3, Anc-FLOdc x2, BLOsc x1, Anc-FLOdc x3, BLOsc x1, Anc-FLOdc x2, BLOsc x3, Anc-FLOdc x1, BLOsc x2, change to Color F, BLOsc x1, Anc-FLOdc x1, BLOsc x1, Anc-FLOdc x7, BLOsc x1, Anc-FLOdc x1, BLOsc x1*, repeat across, BLOsc x1, EBS in last.

Row 15: With Color A, BBS in 1st, *FLOdc x1, BLOsc x13, FLOdc x1, BLOsc x2, FLOdc x1, BLOsc x13, FLOdc x1, BLOsc x2, FLOdc x1, BLOsc x13*, repeat across, FLOdc x1, EBS in last.

*Row 16: With Color E and carrying Colors C & F, BBS in 1st, ***BLOsc x1, Anc-FLOdc x3, BLOsc x1, Anc-FLOdc x5, BLOsc x1, Anc-FLOdc x3**, change to **Color C, BLOsc x1, Anc-FLOdc x1, BLOsc x2, Anc-FLOdc x2, BLOsc x1, Anc-FLOdc x3, BLOsc x1, Anc-FLOdc x3, BLOsc x1, Anc-FLOdc x2, BLOsc x2, Anc-FLOdc x1**, change to **Color F, BLOsc x1, Anc-FLOdc x1, BLOsc x1, Anc-FLOdc x1, BLOsc x1, Anc-FLOdc x2, BLOsc x1, Anc-FLOdc x2, BLOsc x1, Anc-FLOdc x1, BLOsc x1, Anc-FLOdc x1***, repeat across, BLOsc x1, EBS in last.

Row 17: With Color A, BBS in 1st, *FLOdc x1, BLOsc x13, FLOdc x1, BLOsc x2, FLOdc x1, BLOsc x13, FLOdc x1, BLOsc x2, FLOdc x1, BLOsc x13*, repeat across, FLOdc x1, EBS in last.

*Row 18: With Color E and carrying Colors C & F, BBS in 1st, ***BLOsc x1, Anc-FLOdc x4, BLOsc x1, Anc-FLOdc x3, BLOsc x1, Anc-FLOdc x4, BLOsc x1**, change to **Color C, BLOsc x1, Anc-FLOdc x1, BLOsc x3, Anc-FLOdc x2, BLOsc x1, Anc-FLOdc x3, BLOsc x1, Anc-FLOdc x2, BLOsc x3, Anc-FLOdc x1, BLOsc x2**, change to **Color F, BLOsc x1, Anc-FLOdc x1, BLOsc x1, Anc-FLOdc x7, BLOsc x1, Anc-FLOdc x1, BLOsc x1***, repeat across, BLOsc x1, EBS in last.

Row 19: With Color A, BBS in 1st, *FLOdc x1, BLOsc x4, FLOdc x1, BLOsc x3, FLOdc x1, BLOsc x4, FLOdc x2, BLOsc x3, FLOdc x1, BLOsc x9, FLOdc x1, BLOsc x3, FLOdc x3, BLOsc x11, FLOdc x1*, repeat across, FLOdc x1, EBS in last.

*Row 20: With Color E and carrying Colors C & F, BBS in 1st, ***BLOsc x2, Anc-FLOdc x2, BLOsc x3, Anc-FLOdc x1, BLOsc x3, Anc-FLOdc x2, BLOsc x2**, change to **Color C, BLOsc x3, Anc-FLOdc x1, BLOsc x3, Anc-FLOdc x2, BLOsc x1, Anc-FLOdc x2, BLOsc x3, Anc-FLOdc x1, BLOsc x4**, change to **Color F, BLOsc x4, Anc-FLOdc x1, BLOsc x1, Anc-FLOdc x1, BLOsc x1, Anc-FLOdc x1, BLOsc x4***, repeat across, BLOsc x1, EBS in last.

Section 9-Flower Garden

Row 21: With Color A, BBS in 1st, *FLOdc x2, BLOsc x2, FLOdc x3, BLOsc x1, FLOdc x3, BLOsc x2, FLOdc x5, BLOsc x3, FLOdc x1, BLOsc x5, FLOdc x1, BLOsc x3, FLOdc x8, BLOsc x5, FLOdc x4*, repeat across, FLOdc x1, EBS in last.

*Row 22: With Color E and carrying Colors C & F, BBS in 1st, *BLOsc x2, Anc-FLOdc x1, BLOsc x9, Anc-FLOdc x1, BLOsc x2, change to Color C, BLOsc x5, Anc-FLOdc x1, BLOsc x7, Anc-FLOdc x1, BLOsc x6, change to Color F, BLOsc x5, Anc-FLOdc x1, BLOsc x1, Anc-FLOdc x1, BLOsc x5*, repeat across, BLOsc x1, EBS in last.

Row 23: With Color A, BBS in 1st, *FLOdc x2, BLOsc x1, FLOdc x9, BLOsc x1, FLOdc x7, BLOsc x9, FLOdc x11, BLOsc x3, FLOdc x5*, repeat across, FLOdc x1, EBS in last.

Section 10-Envelope Border

The Envelope Border (sometimes called a "double border") is made by crocheting 2 differen borders - on on the backside and another on the frontside - and them seaming them toegether to hide the ends along the sides.

Scan for a
Video Tutorial
from a different project

Back Border

Round 1: With Color A, sc in the FLO of any stitch along the bottom of blanket, sc in FLO in each stitch. In each corner, *sc in FLO, ch 2, sc in FLO.* Along the side, sc through both legs of the border stitches. Invisible join to first stitch. (see below)

Round 2: With Color A, Ch 1, BLOsc in each stitch around. In each corner ch-2 space, *BLOsc, ch 2, BLOsc* in each corner. Invisible join to 1st stitch.

Round 3: With Color B, Ch 1, BLOdc in each stitch around. In each corner ch-2 space, *BLOdc, ch2, BLOdc* in each corner. Invisible join to 1st stitch.

Round 4: With Color A, Repeat Round 2

Section 10-Envelope Border

Invisible Join

- Work last stitch
- Remove hook from loop.
- Insert hook through back of 1st stitch of row
- Grab dropped loop
- Pull yarn loop though.
- Untangle hook & yarn.

Front Border

Round 1: With Color B, Repeat Round 1 of Back Border. Fasten off. Join with Color C.

Round 2-5: Repeat Round 2 of Back Border. Fasten off and join Colors D-F (one color per round).
.

Finishing

- Secure ends by tying two together along each side.
- Trim ends to about 1inch in length.
- With Color C, BLOsc through BOTH borders. (The loops that are closest together on the blanket), ensuring that the ends are enclosed in the envelope border.
- Fasten off.
- Weave in (or hide) all ends.

Thank you
and happy crocheting

Thank you so much for crocheting with me. I know it felt like a labor of love & I hope you loved the process!

Please share pictures of the blanket on all the social media. Tag @juniperandoakes and use #MosaicFlowerGardenCAL and #juniperandoakes so I can see it.

Stay Connected.

Join my email newsletter.

Be the first to know about my new mosaic crochet patterns, discover handy yarn-related products, and join in on my community crochetalongs.

Scan for BONUS crochet pattern
Mosaic ZigZag Blanket

Acknowledgements:

The first "Thank you" always goes to my husband Kameron. Thanks for being my #1 supporter & teammate! (We should get jerseys.)

Thank you to my kids B.G.P. I love you to the moon.

Thank you Mom for teaching me how to crochet. I would not be here without you.

Thank you Sheri for being a fabulous crocheter. Without you, this blanket would not be what is now. You are the one responsible for the fabulous colors and for daring me to try out a new technique. Thanks for pushing me to be a better designer!

Thank you Teri for putting this put together so we could get it out for the re-run of the crochetalong on the blog. I've said it before...You are a super hero.

Thank you Amanda for helping me with the re-run of the CAL. I could not do it without you.

Thank you Mary Maxim for sending me the yarn to use for this blanket.

And a huge thank you to the Juniper & Oakes Crochet Community & the Crazy Yarn Ladies in my membership group. Thank you for believing in me and for being part of my little yarny corner of the internet. It is always such a surprise and absolute treasure to see crocheters around the world crocheting the patterns I put out into the void.

Happy Crocheting!

Overlay Mosaic Crochet
CHEAT SHEET
Juniper&Oakes

Charts are worked from bottom to top.

Worked from right to left on Right Side only.

Every row worked in a different color.

Fasten off at the end of each row.

Stitches Involved

Blank boxes (sc) are worked in BLO of previous row.

X-filled boxes (dc) are worked in FLO of stitch 2 rows below.

Video Tutorial

Scan me

BBS 7 EBS: Every row begins & ends with a sc through the post (or the 'v') of the stitch below, ensuring that both legs on the WS of the stitch are secured to the outside edge.

A	BBS using Color Indicated
	BLOsc
X	FLOdc
+	EBS
	Repeat Across

Mosaic Flower Garden

Mosaic Flower Garden Blanket
Coloring Page
Visualize your perfect color scheme!

www.ingramcontent.com/pod-product-compliance
Lightning Source LLC
Chambersburg PA
CBHW041617120626
46551CB00003B/482